Signposts to Science
Book 6

LIGHT & SOUND

Peter D. Riley

Dryad Press Limited   London

 CONTENTS

© Peter D. Riley 1987
First published 1987

Typeset by Tek-Art Ltd, Kent
and printed in Great Britain by
R.J. Acford
Chichester, Sussex
for the Publishers,
Dryad Press Limited,
8 Cavendish Square,
London W1M 0AJ

ISBN 0 8521 9635 0

ACKNOWLEDGMENTS

The Author and Publishers thank the following for their kind permission to reproduce copyright illustrations: Biophoto Associates, pages 24, 32; Craswell Scientific Limited, page 7; Dartington Glass, page 4; Hoechst, pages 13, 27; R.E. Howarth, page 12; Ilford, pages 16, 17; Monitor Audio Ltd, page 37; National Maritime Museum, London, page 10; Optical Information Council, page 19; Prior Scientific Instruments, Bishop's Stortford, page 5; P.T. Robbins, page 29; The Royal Institute for the Deaf, page 30; TeleFocus: a British Telecom photograph, page 41; Derek Whitford, C.Chem. M.R.S.C., pages 8, 9, 14, 18, 20, 22, 34, 35, 36, 38, 42. The diagrams for the book were drawn by N.R. Williamson.

Cover photograph: British Telecom's "spider-man" engineer installing an optical fibre cable. (TeleFocus: a British Telecom photograph).

INTRODUCTION

Light and sound are so important to our way of life that we usually take them for granted. Only when we have to carefully pick our way to a seat in a dark cinema or search for a book in a quiet library do we perhaps think about light or sound at all. For the rest of the time our brain is too busy *using* the information from the light and sound around us, in order to help us to go about our daily lives – crossing a street, learning something new in class or playing badminton, football or hockey after school.

If you have ever watched a distant thunderstorm you will have discovered that light and sound travel at different speeds. The flash of the lightning is followed a short time later by the rumble of thunder, and yet both were made at the same time – when a current of electricity passed through the air. You may have counted the seconds between seeing the flash and hearing the thunder and worked out how close you were to the storm. Each second between the flash and the thunder stands for one fifth of a mile (or one third of a kilometre).

Light and sound are different in other ways, too, and so they are dealt with separately in this book. In the first part of the book I have tried to give a simple account of light – from the different ways it is made, by hot gases in a star or by chemical reactions in a firefly, for example, to its use in making laser beams and holograms. The second part of the book deals with sound – from the simple rattle made by twanging a ruler on a desk top to the wide range of uses of ultrasonics, for checking metal products in industry, for instance, or examining babies as they grow inside their mothers.

A time scale of scientific discovery and invention relating to light and sound is on page 44 and may be used with most topics to provide some historical background to the subject being studied.

At the end of each double page is a list of further reading suggestions, and at the end of the book is a page of projects. The simplest projects involve only information in this book. The more complex projects involve the use of several books in the series. Other books in the series are referred to throughout by their number, 1 to 7. The books in the series are:

Book 1 Air and Gases
Book 2 Water and Oil
Book 3 The Earth and Space
Book 4 Materials
Book 5 Electricity and Magnetism
Book 6 Light and Sound
Book 7 Science and Life

Sunlight

The sun gives out huge amounts of energy every second. This energy travels through space in the form of waves, called electromagnetic waves. Diagram 1 shows the features of a wave. Electromagnetic waves can be divided into groups by measuring their wavelengths. Table 1 shows the different groups of electromagnetic waves that the sun gives out. You can see from the table that only a small range of electromagnetic waves carry light energy.

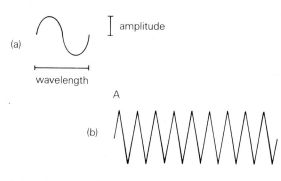

1 The features of a wave
   (a) Wavelength and amplitude
   (b) Frequency. The frequency is the number of waves that pass a point (A in the diagram) in one second.

Table 1   The groups of electromagnetic waves

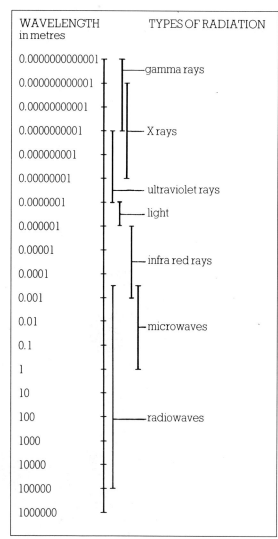

The longest light waves make red light and the shortest waves make violet. In between these are the wavelengths for orange, yellow, green, blue and indigo. In sunlight these wavelengths are mixed together and make white light. An electric lamp also produces a mixture of light waves but these make a more yellow light than sunlight.

Luminous matter

Light and heat

When they are heated strongly, many substances begin to give out light energy and are said to glow or become incandescent. Materials which behave in this way are called incandescent materials.

4

Some examples of incandescent materials
gases – in stars and street lamps.
liquids – lava from the mouth of a volcano.
solids – the tungsten filament in a light bulb and the carbon atoms in the candle flame (see book 1 page 40).

Cool light
If a substance makes light with hardly any heat it is called a luminescent material. There are three kinds of luminescence:

(1) *Phosphorescence* occurs when a substance glows after light has been shone on it. Luminous paint on a watch or clock face is an example of a phosphorescent material.
(2) *Fluorescence* occurs when a substance releases light only when light is shining on it. See book 5 page 21.
(3) *Bioluminescence* is made by living things. See page 24.

Polarized light
When a wave moves up and down, as shown in diagram 1, it is said to vibrate. There are many waves in a light beam and they vibrate in all directions, as diagram 2(a) shows. If this light beam shines on a piece of polarizing material, such as tourmaline, only one light wave will pass through – the others are filtered out. Diagram 2(b) shows a light beam which has passed through a piece of polarizing material.

Uses of polarized light
Polaroid sunglasses reduce the amount of light reaching the eyes and make objects with shiny surfaces easier to see.

Mineral testing. Rocks are made from crystals of different minerals (see book 3 page 16). The crystals are usually very small, transparent and without colour. The microscope in the photograph can be used to test a specimen of a thin slice of rock in the following way. The slide carrying the specimen is placed on the stage (see page 13). A beam of polarized light is passed from the hole in the stage, through the specimen and into the eyepiece. When the crystals are looked at through the eyepiece many of them may appear to be coloured. The colours made by the different crystals can be used to help identify the minerals.

Further reading

TOPIC	BOOK	PAGE
Refraction	6	8
Light from living things	6	24
Minerals	3	18
Lighting	5	20

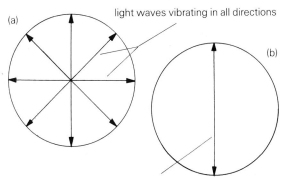

light waves vibrating in all directions

(a)

(b)

light wave vibrating in only one direction

2 End view of a light beam
   (a) Normal light beam
   (b) Polarized light beam

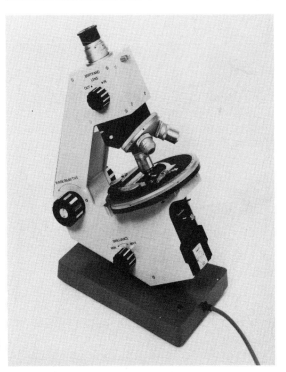

We see nearly everything around us by reflected light. For example, the trees on page 22 are seen by the light they reflect from the sun, the eye on page 18 is seen by the light it reflects from the flash ring on the camera, and the candle wax and holder (page 4) are seen by the light they reflect from the candle flame above them. The sun, flash ring and candle flame are luminous (see page 4). The objects around them, that we see by reflected light, are non-luminous.

Types of reflections

Diffuse reflections are the most common type. You can see these words because diffuse reflections are taking place now on the surface of this page. Most surfaces, like this paper, have many tiny hollows and projections. When a beam of parallel light rays strikes the surface the rays are reflected in all directions, as diagram 3 shows.

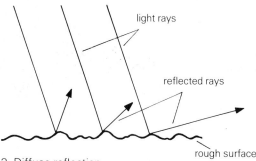

3 Diffuse reflection

Specular reflections take place on very smooth surfaces like mirrors or polished metal. When a beam of parallel light rays strikes the smooth surface, the reflected rays are parallel too.

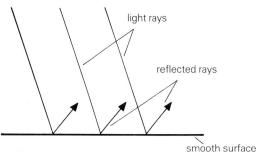

4 Specular reflection

Reflex reflections are made by special materials (see diagram 5) which are used for clothing, road signs and vehicle number plates in Britain. The reflectors on the backs of vehicles such as cars and trucks have a special design. When the headlamp beam of a following car strikes them, they reflect the light upwards to the driver's face. This makes the reflectors easier to see in the dark.

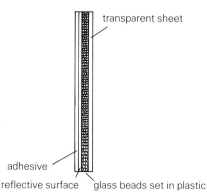

5 Section through a reflective material

Mirrors

Mirrors are usually made of glass with a shiny metal coating, called the silver, on one side.

Flat mirrors reflect light as shown in diagram 4. The light rays appear to be coming from a picture of the object behind the mirror (see diagram 6). This picture is called a virtual image. It is the same size as the object, but the features on the image are arranged on the opposite side to those on the object, as you can see when you look in a mirror.

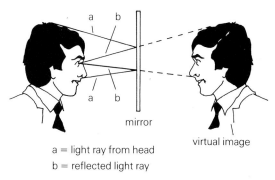

a = light ray from head
b = reflected light ray

6 Reflection in a flat mirror

Concave mirror (diagram 7). When a beam of light strikes a concave mirror the rays are directed to a point in front of the mirror, called the principal focus. If your face is placed between the principal focus and the mirror's surface a magnified virtual image is made, as diagram 7(b) shows. This image is particularly useful if you want to examine an area of skin on your face and for helping people to shave or put on make-up.

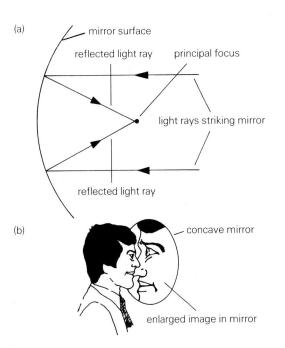

7 Reflection in a concave mirror

An object at a great distance from a concave mirror forms a real image, as shown in the diagram of the telescope on page 11.

The *parabolic mirror* (diagram 8) is used in headlamps to reflect light from the bulb into a beam of parallel rays.

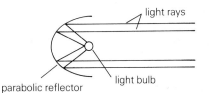

8 Reflection in a car headlamp

GLOSSARY

light beam: light energy moving in one particular direction.
light ray: the straight line path made by light waves.
virtual image: an image which appears to be behind a mirror.

Convex mirrors like those in the photograph reflect light beams so that they make a virtual image, smaller than the object, and give a wide field of view. The image made by the mirror on the ceiling at the right, for example, gives an almost complete view of the room. Mirrors like these are placed in stores to help sales assistants look out for thieves. Smaller convex mirrors are used on all kinds of vehicles to help give the driver a wide view of the road behind.

Further reading

TOPIC	BOOK	PAGE
Telescopes	6	10
The microscope	6	12
Holograms	6	21
Lasers	6	26

REFRACTION

Air and glass are both transparent substances. Glass is a much denser substance than air (see book 1 page 5). Diagram 9 shows how light rays change direction when they pass through substances which have different densities. This changing direction or bending of light rays is called refraction.

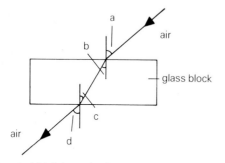

a, c = angles at which light rays strike surface between air and glass
b, d = angles of refraction

9 Refraction of light through a glass block

The prism (diagram 10)
A beam of sunlight contains a mixture of light waves which make the seven colours mentioned on page 4. The waves travel at the same speed through air, but when they pass into glass they slow down. The waves with the shorter wavelengths slow down more than the waves with the longer wavelengths and this makes the beam spread out, as shown in the diagram. When the light leaves the prism it is refracted again and the waves are spread out even more, to form a spectrum. The arrows on diagram 10 mark the positions of the colours, in the spectrum which forms on the screen.

10 Refraction through a prism

GLOSSARY

element: a substance which cannot be broken down into a more simple substance; e.g. carbon.
spectrum: a band of different colours which is made when light waves have been separated into different wavelengths; e.g. a rainbow.

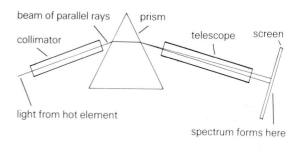

11 Parts of a spectroscope

The spectroscope (diagram 11)
When an element is heated strongly, it gives out light. If the light is passed through a spectroscope, the collimator makes the beam into parallel rays, which all strike the prism at the same angle, and the telescope makes the refracted light produce a large spectrum which can be easily examined. Each element can be identified by the spectrum it makes, just as you can be identified by your fingerprints.

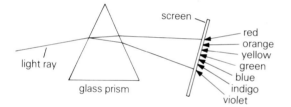

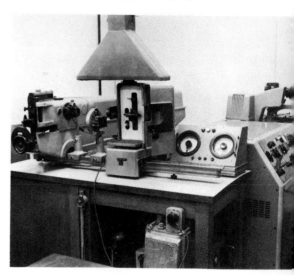

The *optical spectroscope* shown in the photograph on page 8 is used in industry to identify the elements in a material. The material is heated in the box, shown open, in the centre of the bench. Light from the hot material passes through the lenses on the left and into the long metal box, where a prism is kept. The spectrum made by the prism is photographed in the long box and this photograph is then examined with the microscope on the right.

Lenses

A lens is a piece of glass or plastic which makes a beam of light rays come together (converge), as shown in diagram 12, or spread out (diverge), as shown in diagram 13. Each part of a lens can be thought to behave like a prism, as the diagrams show. By carefully moving the lens in front of an object, a larger or smaller image can be made.

12 A converging lens

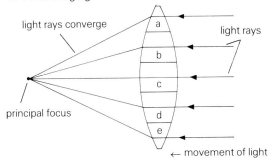

a, b, c, d, e = parts of lens which act like a prism

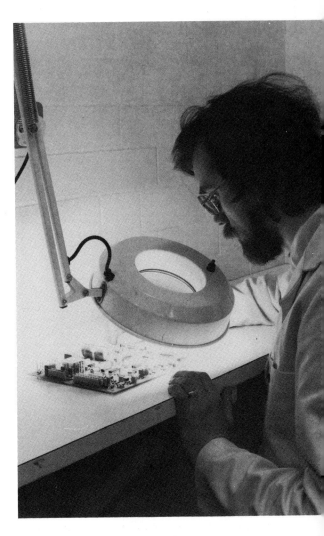

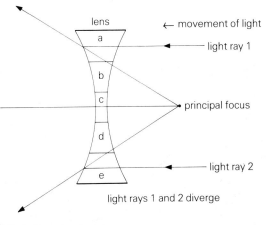

13 A diverging lens

The convex lens in the photograph, for example, is being used to make a larger image of the pieces of electronic equipment, so that the engineer can carefully check the way the pieces have been joined together.

Further reading

Objects, images and the eye

There are millions of cells in the eye which are sensitive to light (see page 18). When an image of an object forms in the eye (see diagram 14), some of the cells send information to the brain and we see the object.

A *nearby object* (diagram 14) makes a large image. A great number of cells send information to the brain, and a large, clear view of many features on the object is seen.

A *distant object* (diagram 15) makes a smaller image. Fewer cells send information to the brain, and a smaller view of the object, showing fewer features, is seen.

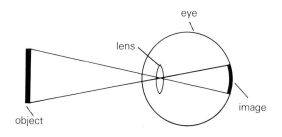

14 Seeing a nearby object

15 Seeing a distant object

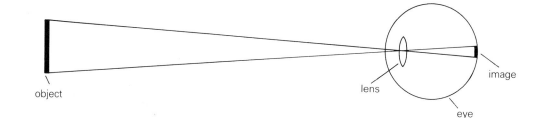

The light rays reaching the eye from a *very distant object* are parallel. They may form a very tiny image if the object is bright, but if the object is dim they will not form an image at all.

Telescopes

The purpose of the telescope is to collect enough light from a distant or very distant object and focus the rays so that they make a large image in the eye. This can be done by refraction or reflection.

Refracting telescopes

The *astronomical telescope* in the photograph is being used in an astronomer's observatory. The path of the light rays through the telescope is shown in diagram 16. The light rays coming from the magnified image X enter the eye and make a large image inside it. The magnified image X is upside down. This does not really matter for studying objects in space, but in telescopes made for use by sailors or birdwatchers, for example, a third lens is added. This extra lens turns image X the right way up.

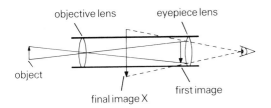

16 The astronomical telescope

Opera glasses (diagram 17) are really a pair of Galilean telescopes (see page 44). They make an image which is 2½-3 times the size of the object.

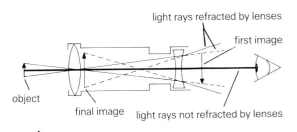

▲
17 Opera glasses

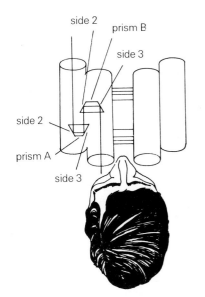

18 Binoculars

Binoculars (diagram 18) are telescopes which have been shortened by using prisms. When light enters prism A, it is reflected off side 2 to side 3, then on to prism B, where it is reflected off sides 2 and 3 before it enters the eyepiece. The prisms are arranged so that they make an image which is the right way up.

The limit of a refracting telescope
A refracting telescope is made more powerful by fitting larger lenses. A very large lens is difficult to support and its weight squashes some parts of the glass and stretches other parts. When light passes through these damaged parts it forms a blurred, useless image.

The reflecting telescope (diagram 19)
A large concave mirror is easier to support than a large lens, and so the most powerful telescopes have a concave mirror to collect the light and focus it to make an image, as the diagram shows. A plane (flat) mirror is placed at the point where the image forms. It reflects the image into the eyepiece. The lenses in the eyepiece magnify the image from space, so that it makes a large image in the eye.

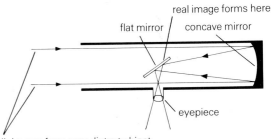

19 The reflecting telescope

Further reading

THE MICROSCOPE

The microscope in the photograph on the right is being used to examine some very tiny organisms. They can be seen on the television screen in the background. Where is the television camera?

How the microscope works

When you look at a very tiny object, the light rays coming from it make a very small image in your eye, as diagram 20 shows. This small image lets us see only a few features on the object.

If the tiny object is viewed through a microscope, the light rays are refracted, as shown in diagram 21. The magnified final image Y makes a large image in the eye and many features of the object can be seen.

Specimens for the microscope

A *small specimen* is placed on a strip of glass, called a slide, and covered with a mountant and a thin glass cover slip, as diagram 22 shows.

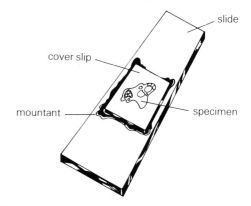

22 A mounted specimen for the microscope

GLOSSARY

mountant: a transparent liquid or solid which supports the specimen on the slide.

---

20 (Left) The eye and a very small object

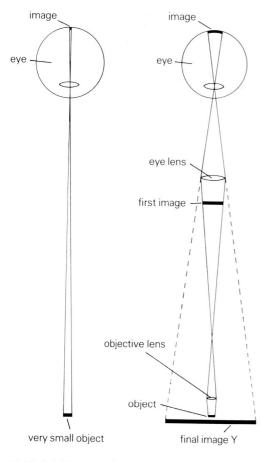

21 (Right) The eye, the microscope and a very small object

A *large specimen* is placed in a wax block and sliced on a microtome, like the one in the photograph on page 12. You can see the large, dark specimen held in a wax block above a horizontal metal blade. This is razor-sharp. When the specimen is moved down, a thin slice of the specimen and wax is cut off the block. A ribbon of 10 slices is being held up from the blade. Each slice will be placed on a slide and mounted, as shown in diagram 22.

The parts of a microscope (diagram 23)
The *stage* supports the slide.
The *stage clips* hold the slide in position.
The *mirror* reflects light from a bench lamp or sunless sky – NEVER FROM THE SUN. If light directly from the sun was focused into the eye the retina (see page 18) would be destroyed.
The *objective lens mounting* contains a number of lenses, like the ones shown in diagram 25 on page 14. The arrangement of the lenses helps to make a clear, bright first image.
The *eyepiece* contains two lenses, which magnify the first image and make the final image easy to view when the eye is brought close to the top of the microscope.

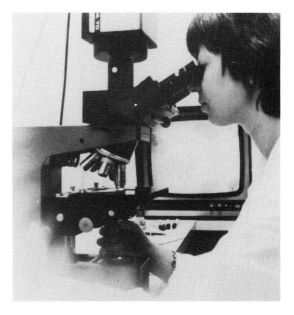

The *focusing control* is turned to raise the stage and bring the slide closer to the objective lens mounting. When the operator is looking down the microscope, as in the photograph here, the control is turned again and the stage is lowered until a clear image of the specimen is seen.

Lighting the specimen
Transmitted light is light that is shone through the specimen from below the stage, as in the photograph. *Reflected light* is light that is shone onto the specimen from above, as shown in the photograph on page 20.

Most specimens, such as the cells in plants and animals, are examined by transmitted light. The surfaces of larger specimens, such as pieces of metal, are examined by reflected light.

Light can only be used to make clear images up to about 2000 times magnification. Much greater magnifications are made with an electron microscope (see further reading).

Further reading

TOPIC	BOOK	PAGE
Reflections	6	6
Refraction	6	8
Electron microscopes	5	34

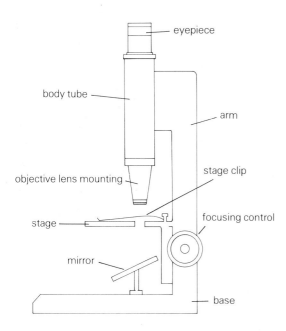

23 The parts of a microscope

eyepiece

body tube

arm

objective lens mounting

stage clip

stage

focusing control

mirror

base

How a simple camera works

The film is held in a light-tight box, as diagram 24 shows. When the button is pressed, a piece of metal called a shutter moves away from the hole behind the lens and lets rays of light reach the film.

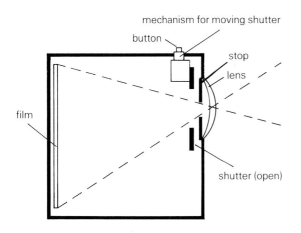

24 A simple camera

The *lens* can only focus light coming from certain distances. If an object is too close to the lens, the light rays make a blurred image on the film.

The *shutter* controls how much light reaches the film in a certain time. Most simple shutters expose the film to light for 1/30th to 1/50th of a second. If a fast-moving object is photographed at one of these shutter speeds, a blurred image will form on the film. This image forms because the object has travelled a large distance between the moment the shutter opened and the moment it closed. Only still or slow-moving objects can be photographed clearly with a simple camera.

The *stop* controls the amount of light which passes through the lens. In a simple camera, the single lens may have faults around its edge. If light passed through these faults before reaching the film, a blurred image would be made. A stop with a small opening is fitted to a simple camera, so that only light from the centre of the lens reaches the film. Simple cameras must be used in bright conditions if enough light is to reach the film and make a clear photograph.

The adjustable camera

The camera in this photograph can be adjusted to take clear photographs in a wide range of light conditions, from dim to very bright. It can also take photographs of fast-moving objects like the motor bike on page 29.

The *lens mounting* at the front of the camera holds a number of lenses, as diagram 25 shows. This arrangement of lenses makes a very clear image, which can be focused on to the film.

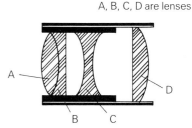

A, B, C, D are lenses

25 The lens mounting in an adjustable camera

There are three rings on the lens mounting. Each ring has a set of numbers on it. When the ring with the widely spaced numbers is turned, the lenses move and the camera can be sharply focused. When the middle ring is turned, the size of the opening in the stop is changed. In dim conditions the opening is increased to let more light reach the film. In very bright conditions the opening is made smaller to prevent too much light reaching the film and spoiling the photograph.

The ring nearest the front of the mounting controls the speed at which the shutter opens and closes. The period of time that the shutter is open is called the exposure time. By turning this ring, any one of ten speeds can be selected – from a one-second exposure to a 1/500th-second exposure.

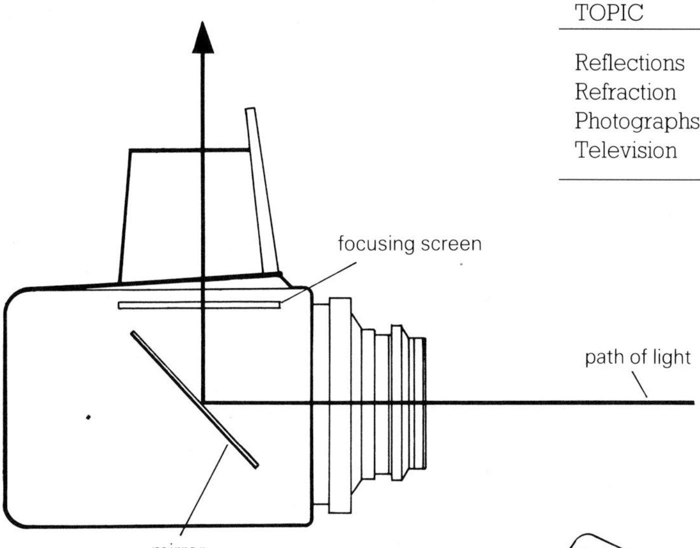

If you were to look down the *viewfinder* on the top of this camera, you would see the light coming through the lenses, as diagram 26 shows. In many types of adjustable camera the light passes through a special prism (see diagram 27). In both these types of camera, when the shutter is opened, the mirror in front of it is raised so that the light passes straight to the film.

Further reading

TOPIC	BOOK	PAGE
Reflections	6	6
Refraction	6	8
Photographs	6	16
Television	5	28

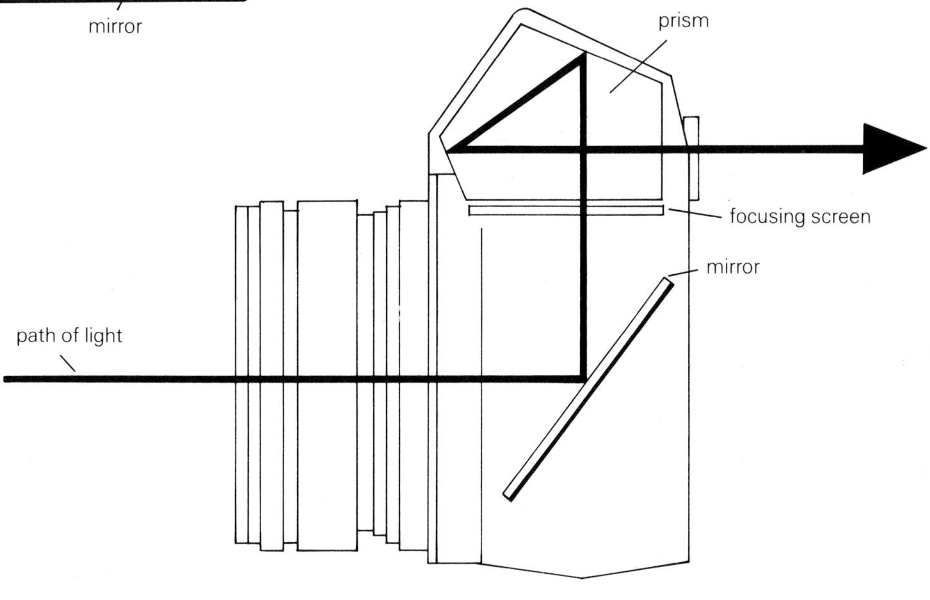

26 The viewfinder of an adjustable camera (Type 1)

focusing screen

path of light

mirror

prism

to the eye

focusing screen

mirror

path of light

27 The viewfinder of an adjustable camera (Type 2)

28 A piece of film

gelatin

plastic strip

halide crystals

Film

A piece of film is shown in diagram 28. Some silver halide crystals magnified 20,000 times by an electron microscope are shown in the first of the two photographs below.

If a flag like the one shown in diagram 29 is photographed, many light rays from the white cross strike the region of the film marked A in diagram 30. In this region the light makes large numbers of silver halide crystals produce a little silver metal. Few light rays from the dark part of the flag strike region B, and so few crystals here make any silver.

GLOSSARY

developing tank: a special tank which allows liquids to enter and leave without light getting in.

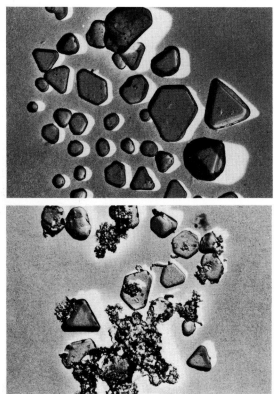

29 A flag – the subject of a photograph

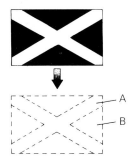

A

B

30 The film on which the image of the flag is made

Developing a black and white film

The film is wound into a coil (diagram 31) in the dark, then placed in a developing tank (diagram 32). A liquid containing a mixture of chemicals (called the developer) is poured into the tank. Chemical reactions take place between the developer and all the crystals which have made a little silver. The developer makes these crystals produce more silver. The bottom-left photograph shows the silver made by crystals which have been treated with developer for 16 seconds. Usually the developer is left in the tank for about five minutes. The tank is shaken occasionally to make sure that air bubbles do not settle on the film and stop the developer reaching the crystals.

All the developer is poured out of the tank and a fixer is added. This liquid dissolves the halide crystals which did not make any silver when the film was exposed to light.

Then the fixer is poured out of the tank, and the film is washed and hung up to dry. The picture of the flag appears as shown in diagram 33, and is called a negative.

31 The coil of film on a spool

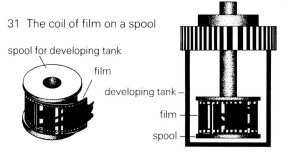

spool for developing tank

film

developing tank

film

spool

32 The spool in the developing tank

33 The negative of the flag

34 The enlarger

(a)
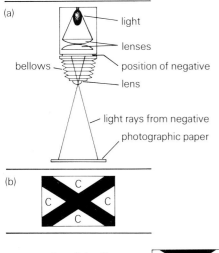
light

lenses

bellows

position of negative

lens

light rays from negative

photographic paper

(b)

C C C C

35 The print of the flag

Printing a negative

The photograph on the right shows a laboratory set up to make prints from negatives. A safe light (mounted on the wall in this laboratory) gives out enough light to let the photographer see to print the negative, yet does not give out too much light which might spoil the developing prints.

The equipment which looks like a box on a stand, with a white tray below it, is called an enlarger. Diagram 34(a) shows parts of a simple enlarger. The bellows of the enlarger in the photograph have been squashed close together. The negative is placed in the enlarger and a piece of photographic paper is placed in the tray. The photographic paper contains silver halide crystals too. When the lamp in the enlarger is switched on, light from the negative is focused on the photographic paper. Most of the crystals in the regions marked C (diagram 34b) make small amounts of silver. Few crystals in the cross-shaped region make silver.

The paper is then developed in a similar way to the negative, but the chemicals and apparatus on the front bench of the laboratory are used. The finished print of the flag is shown in diagram 35.

Colour photographs

There are three layers of silver halide crystals in a colour film. The top layer makes an image from the blue light it receives, the middle layer makes an image from green light, and the bottom layer makes an image from red light. Special dyes are used to develop the film. The negative is printed onto paper which also has three layers of crystals. Each layer is sensitive to a particular colour of light. The final image we see in the colour print is made from the three coloured images which formed on the film when the photograph was taken.

Further reading

TOPIC	BOOK	PAGE
Light	6	4
The camera	6	14
Electron microscopes	5	34

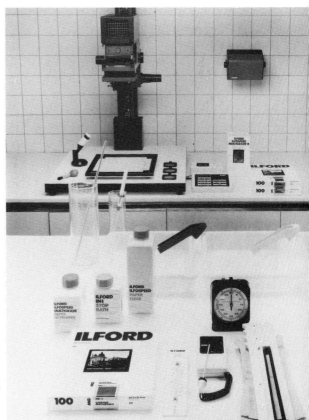

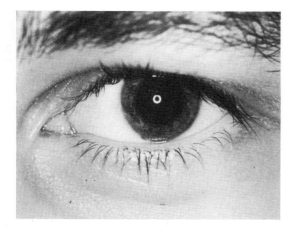

This close-up photograph of an eye was taken using a special ring-like flash bulb. You can see its reflection in the eye's moist surface. The tear glands, under the upper eyelid, make the liquid which covers the eye with a thin film of moisture, and this liquid slowly drains into the tear duct in the left corner. The moisture keeps the front of the eye clean, by carrying away any dust particles that settle there.

The transparent parts of the eye

The *conjunctiva* lies below the film of moisture. It forms a protective surface.

The *cornea* refracts the light towards the pupil

– the black hole in the centre of the eye.

The *aqueous humor* is a liquid which supplies nourishment to the living tissues in the front part of the eye.

The *lens* refracts the light towards the retina.

The *vitreous humor* is a jelly which holds up, or supports, the back part of the eye.

The light controllers (diagrams 36 and 37)

In the photograph you can see a grey ring between the white of the eye and the pupil. This ring is called the iris. It contains two sets of muscles, as diagram 37 shows. If too much light is passing through the pupil, the circular muscles become shorter, the radial muscles relax and become longer, and the pupil is made smaller.

When too little light is entering the pupil, the radial muscles become shorter, the circular muscles relax and become longer, and the pupil increases in size.

Focusing the lens (diagrams 36 and 37)

When the ciliary muscle is relaxed (not working), the lens is squashed nearly flat by the aqueous and vitreous humors. The thin lens focuses light coming from distant objects on to the retina. When the ciliary muscle works, it becomes smaller and pulls in closer to the lens. This action makes the lens thicker and more able to focus on nearby objects.

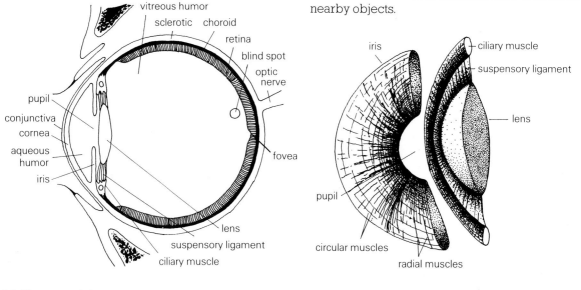

36 The parts of the eye

37 The iris and the lens

The retina

The retina contains millions of cells, which send electrical messages to the brain when light shines on them. The messages travel along fibres which meet at the blind spot and form the optic nerve, which is connected to the brain. The messages are sorted out in the brain, to give us the sensation of sight.

Cone-shaped cells at the fovea let us see clearly and in colour, when the light is bright. Rod-shaped cells in other parts of the retina let us see less clearly and in black and white, when the light is dim.

The eye test

The woman in the photograph on the right is having her eyes tested. She is wearing a special frame which can support a number of lenses. The optician is placing a lens in front of her right eye. He finds the lenses which help his patient see most clearly, by testing her with a number of lenses from his cabinet on the right. Diagram 38 shows how lenses can be used to correct short sight and long sight.

38 Using lenses to correct vision

(a) Correcting short sight

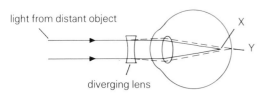

light from distant object

X

Y

diverging lens

(b) Correcting long sight

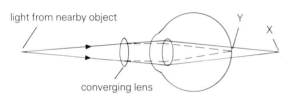

light from nearby object

Y

X

converging lens

X = point were image formed without correcting lens
Y = point were image formed with correcting lens

GLOSSARY

long sight: only being able to see distant objects clearly. It is caused by weak lenses in the eyes, or short eyeballs.
short sight: only being able to see near objects clearly. It is caused by strong lenses in the eyes, or long eyeballs.

Further reading

TOPIC	BOOK	PAGE
Refraction	6	8
The ear	6	30

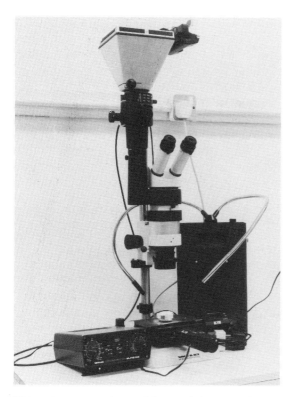

This microscope is used for studying specimens by reflected light (see page 13). On the stage you can see a brightly lit specimen. The light is made inside the black box on the right. It is directed down hundreds of tiny glass threads called optical fibres. The threads are in the two flexible arms which are attached to the top of the box.

Light in an optical fibre (diagram 39)
Many types of fibre are made from two kinds of glass. One kind is used to make the fibre core and the other kind is used to make the sheath around it. If the light rays entering the glass core strike the sheath at a small angle, they are reflected inside, as the diagram shows. The reflected rays pass along the fibre and produce a bright beam of light when they leave. This beam could be used to light a specimen, as in the photograph. If the light entering the fibre hits the sheath at a large angle, the rays escape through the sides and no light beam is formed.

Optical fibres are very thin and can bend. Light rays striking the sheath at a small angle can be reflected around the bends so that the beam leaving the ends of the fibres can be pointed in almost any direction.

A simple fibrescope (diagram 40)
A powerful beam of light is focused by a concave mirror onto the ends of fibres at A. The light travels to B and is reflected from the object into the fibres which lead to the eyepiece. By turning controls close to the eyepiece (not shown in the diagram), the end B can be turned in almost any direction, to give a very wide range of views.

Fibrescopes are used to examine parts of machinery which are difficult to reach, such as the insides of fuel tanks or helicopter blades. They are also used to investigate the insides of bodies (see page 32), such as the lungs and the digestive system.

39 A piece of optical fibre (highly magnified)

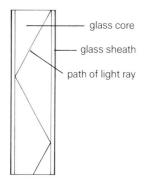

glass core

glass sheath

path of light ray

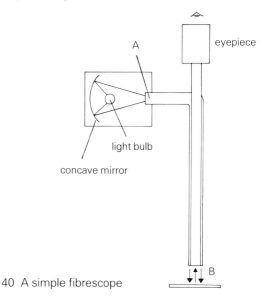

A

eyepiece

light bulb

concave mirror

B

40 A simple fibrescope

20

When you look at an image on a hologram it seems to be solid. You see that it has the three dimensions of length, width and height, as diagram 41 shows. A photograph image (diagram 42) has only two dimensions.

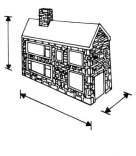

41 The image on a hologram

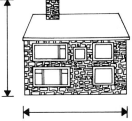

42 The image on a photograph

Making a hologram (diagram 43)

A laser beam (see page 26) is split into two – the reference beam and the reflected or signal beam, as the diagram shows. When the light waves in the reflected beam mix with the light waves in the reference beam they make a pattern on the photographic plate. This is called an interference pattern. The pattern is recorded on the plate just as a picture is recorded on a photograph. This record of the pattern is called a hologram.

The hologram image

If a laser is shone on to the hologram plate at the same angle as the reference beam was shone at the photographic plate in diagram 43, the interference pattern makes a three-dimensional image behind the plate, as diagram 44 shows.

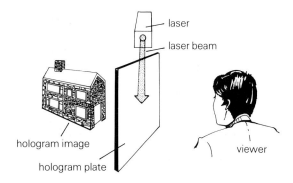

44 The hologram image

Uses of holograms

Information storage. A hologram image can provide almost as much information as the original object, but the hologram is much easier to store – especially if the object is bulky. Many images can be stored on one plate, just by changing the angles of the laser beams.

Engineering. The hologram image of a part in a working machine can be shone onto the same part when the machine is at rest. By looking at the image and the object together, the engineer can see if the part is slightly squashed, stretched or shaken when the machine is working.

Further reading

TOPIC	BOOK	PAGE
Reflections	6	6
Lasers	6	26
Glass	4	10

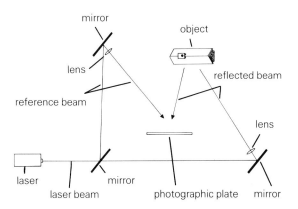

43 Equipment for making a hologram

PLANTS AND LIGHT

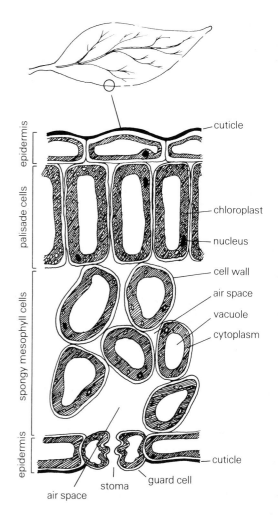

45 The cells in a leaf. (The mechanism of the stomata is explained in book 2).

The sunlight shining into this wood gives the plants energy to make food, helps them grow upwards and makes some of them open their leaves or flowers in the daytime.

The leaf (diagram 45)
Plants make food in their leaves by a process called photosynthesis. Light passes through the clear, waxy cuticle and transparent epidermis cells into the middle part of the leaf. Here, some of the light enters the chloroplasts in the cells. Each chloroplast is packed with molecules of the green pigment called chlorophyll. This pigment absorbs light energy.

Food from light
Leaves make food called carbohydrates (see further reading). The raw materials for making these are water, from the soil, and carbon dioxide, from the air. The energy from light is used to split up the water molecules into hydrogen ions and oxygen molecules. The hydrogen ions are joined with atoms in the

carbon dioxide, in a complicated way, to make carbohydrate molecules, and the oxygen is released into the air.

The growing stem
The stem tip (diagram 46). A plant stem is made from thousands of cells. The cells are made in a

GLOSSARY

auxin: a chemical made by a plant, which helps it to grow.

region near the stem tip, called the growing point. Auxin makes the growing point produce new cells quickly.

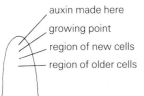

auxin made here
growing point
region of new cells
region of older cells

46 The tip of a shoot

Growing out of the shade. The auxin is destroyed by light. When the stem breaks through the surface of the soil it is usually in dim or dark surroundings, because the rocks and plants close by, like those on the woodland floor, keep it in the shade. As the auxin is not destroyed in these conditions it helps the stem to grow quickly to reach the light, so that the leaves can begin to make food. As the stem grows out of the shade the sunlight begins to destroy the auxin and the stem grows more slowly.

The bending stem. You may have noticed that plants on a windowsill bend towards the light. This happens because the light on the sunny side destroys more auxin than the light on the shady side. Fewer cells are made on the sunny side than on the shady side. The extra cells on the shady side make the stem bend over towards the sunlight, as diagram 47 shows.

shady side   sunny side

auxin not destroyed   auxin destroyed
– it reaches the growing point   – little reaches the growing point

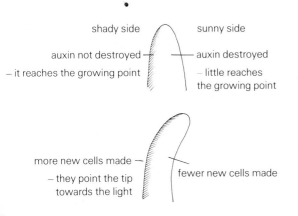

more new cells made
– they point the tip towards the light
fewer new cells made

47 The shoot tip and light

Sleep movements

Light controls the movements of flowers and leaves in some plants. The way the movements are made is very complicated. In many plants the movements are due to the way water is stored in the cells near the leaves or the flowers. Light may make the cells store water, swell up and open the flower, for example. Darkness may make the cells lose water, become soft and close the flower. Diagram 48 shows two examples of sleep movements.

(a) Dandelion (day)   (b) Dandelion (night)

(c) Wood sorrel (day)   (d) Wood sorrel (night)

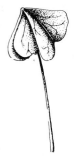

48 Sleep movements

Further reading

TOPIC	BOOK	PAGE
Light	6	4
Water in living things	2	30
Plants for food	7	16

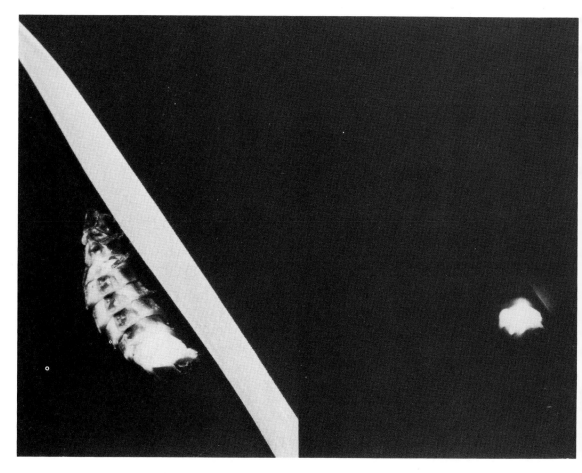

This photograph is really two photographs joined together. The one on the left shows a female glow-worm on a blade of grass. A lamp was being shone onto the animal in order to take the photograph. On the right is a photograph of the same animal, taken after the lamp was switched off. All the light in this picture was made by a chemical reaction taking place inside the animal's body.

Cold light

When light is made by a burning candle (see page 4 and book 1 page 40), or by an electric lamp (book 5 page 20), a great deal of heat energy is produced. If this were to happen inside the glow-worm it would burn itself to death! Very little heat energy is produced in the chemical reaction which makes light in living things, and they shine with a cold glow.

Fireflies and glow-worms

These animals are really beetles. There are 1100 different kinds or species. Most of them live in tropical countries.

Fireflies (diagram 49). Both males and females have well-developed light-making organs, but usually only the male can fly. The males make flashes of light when they fly in the evenings and the females flash back at them. The flashes act as signals to bring the males and females together for mating. Each species can be recognized by the way the males and females flash their signals at each other.

Glow-worm is the name given to the light-making beetle found in Britain. The male has only very small light-making organs, but the wingless female, which looks worm-like, can make a bright light to attract a mate as the photograph shows.

24

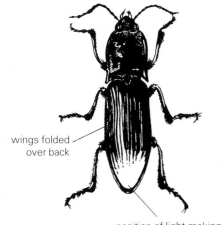

wings folded over back

position of light-making organ

49 Male firefly

comb

51 A comb jelly

Sea animals

Noctiluca (diagram 50) has a body made from a single cell. It has tiny grain-like structures inside it which make light. Large numbers of Noctiluca can be found near the surface of the sea. Their light can make the sea sparkle at night.

0.5 mm

50 Noctiluca

Comb jellies (diagram 51) are species of jellyfish. They swim in the upper waters of the sea by moving their combs up and down. The combs are made from rows of tiny hairs. The combs also make light.

Deep-sea fish (diagram 52). When light passes into water some of the light waves are scattered and some are absorbed by the molecules in the liquid. As the light passes down through sea water, this scattering and absorbing of the light

light-making organs

52 A deep-sea fish

waves make the light weaker until, at a certain depth, it fades away completely, leaving darkness below.

About a thousand species of fish live in this dark water and nearly two thirds of them have organs which make light. These organs are used to help the fish see or to signal to others which are swimming close by.

Further reading

TOPIC	BOOK	PAGE
Light	6	4
Animals in the air	1	16
Microscopic water life	2	10

A ray of light coming from the sun, a candle or an electric lamp has light waves arranged in it as shown in diagram 53. The laser beam has an orderly arrangement of light waves, as in diagram 54. It is the orderly arrangement of light waves in a laser beam that gives it the power to burn through metal or cut holes in diamonds.

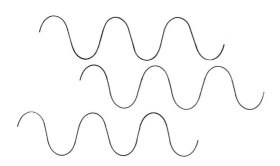

53 Light waves in an ordinary light beam

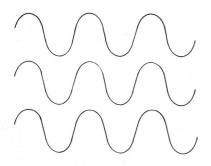

54 Light waves in a laser beam

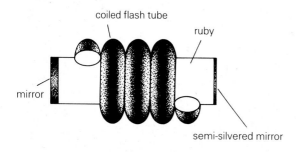

coiled flash tube
ruby
mirror
semi-silvered mirror

55 The main parts of a ruby laser

The ruby laser (diagram 55)

This was the first kind of laser to be made (see page 45). The diagram shows the two important parts of the laser in simple form. The coiled flash tube provides the energy to begin making laser light. The specially made ruby crystal contains chromium ions which have a store of energy that can be released as light waves.

Laser light forms in the following way. The energy in a flash of light from the tube makes a chromium ion in the crystal release its stored energy as a light wave. If the light wave moves through a crystal, as shown in diagram 56, it may strike another chromium ion and make it release its energy as light waves too. As the light waves pass through the crystal they strike more chromium ions and more light waves are released. All the waves are the same length and in the ruby laser they make red light.

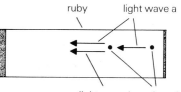

ruby   light wave a

light wave b   chromium atoms

56 Light waves and chromium atoms

The mirrors at the ends of the crystal reflect the light waves, so they pass through the crystal again. They may pass through the crystal many times (see diagram 57). When a large number of light waves have been made, the semi-silvered mirror can no longer reflect them and they pass out of the crystal and form a flash or pulse of laser light which is a million times brighter than sunlight.

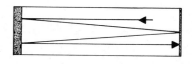

57 The path of light waves through a ruby crystal

Gas lasers

The most common lasers used today have a tube of gas instead of a ruby crystal. They work in a similar way to a ruby laser but make a *beam* of laser light, like the one shown in the photograph, instead of pulses. The helium-neon laser is used in schools to show how lasers work. The carbon dioxide laser makes a beam of light that can destroy rock.

Uses of lasers

Laser beams can be focused like ordinary light beams. The heat at the point of focus can be used in a number of ways, as these examples show:

In industry lasers are used to cut cloth, drill holes in metal or weld pieces of metal together.

In medicine lasers are used to weld detached retinas (see page 18) back into place and to destroy certain kinds of tumours.

Lasers and communications

Laser light can carry messages like radio waves (see book 5 page 26). More messages can be carried by lasers than by radio waves because there are more waves in a laser beam than in a beam of radio waves. Lasers are prevented from working properly in foggy conditions, and so the messages on a laser beam are sent underground in optical fibres (see page 20).

Lasers and holograms

– see page 21.

Further reading

TOPIC	BOOK	PAGE
Reflections	6	6
The eye	6	18
Optical fibres	6	20
Holograms	6	21
Radio	5	26

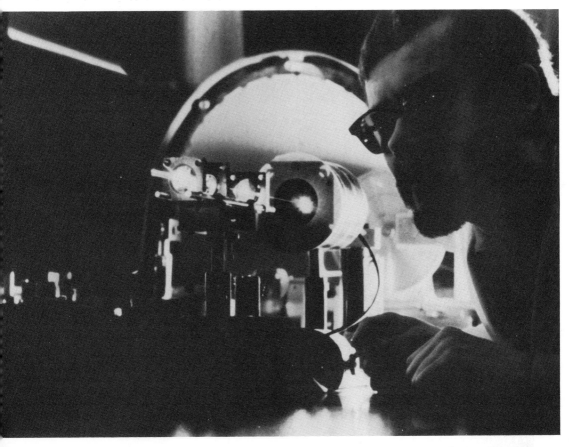

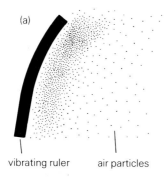

(a) (b)

vibrating ruler   air particles

58 Vibrations and air particles

Most people at school have twanged a ruler on the edge of their desk at some time. When you do this you can see the ruler moving very quickly up and down. This type of movement is called a vibrating movement.

59 Vibrations and sound waves

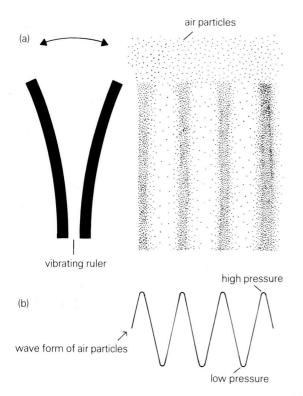

(a)

air particles

vibrating ruler

(b)

high pressure

wave form of air particles

low pressure

When something vibrates it moves the particles of air around it. One moment it pushes on the air particles and squashes them together or compresses them (diagram 58a). This increases the pressure of the air in this region. The next moment the vibrating object pulls away from those air particles and lets them spread out a little (diagram 58b). This spreading-out makes a region of lower pressure.

If the object keeps vibrating, the air particles around it vibrate, too, and pass on the regions of high and low pressure, as diagram 59(a) shows. When these changes in air pressure are plotted on a graph, a wave form is made, like that shown in diagram 59(b). The waves of changing air pressure make the eardrums vibrate too (see page 31). When this happens we say we can hear a sound. These waves, which make our eardrums vibrate, are called sound waves. A sound wave which moves through the air as described here is called a progressive wave.

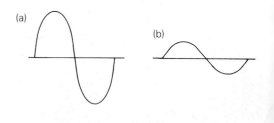

(a) (b)

60 (a) Wave form of a loud sound
   (b) Wave form of a quiet sound

lower frequency sound waves higher frequency sound waves

61 The Doppler effect

Loud sounds (diagram 60a)

When something makes large vibrations, like the loudspeakers at a pop concert for example, the air particles are greatly compressed and spread out, making sound waves as shown in the diagram.

Quiet sounds (diagram 60b)

A ticking watch makes small vibrations and the air around it is only slightly compressed and spread out, making small waves as shown in the diagram.

The pitch of a sound

The pitch of a sound is made by the number of waves that pass from its vibrating body in a second. The number of waves per second is called the frequency and is measured in hertz. A frequency of one wave per second is 1 hertz. A low-pitched sound, such as that made by a fog

horn, has a low frequency of 30 or 40 hertz. The high-pitched sound of a whistle has a large frequency of 15,000 hertz.

The Doppler effect (diagram 61)

The motor bike in the photograph has a side-car attached to it, on the other side. (What parts of the side-car rider can you see as the motor bike races into a right-hand bend?) When the motor bike rushed by, the photographer heard the pitch of the engine sound change. You may have heard a similar change happen when an ambulance with sirens blaring rushed past you.

As the ambulance speeds towards you the sound waves from its siren are squashed together and this raises their frequency or pitch. When the ambulance rushes away from you the sound waves spread out more and the frequency falls. The Doppler effect is the term that is used to describe the pitch change which is made when a noisy object passes by.

The speed of sound

Sound travels through the air at 764 mph when the air temperature is 15°C. If the air is warmer the sound travels faster; if the air is cooler it travels more slowly.

Further reading

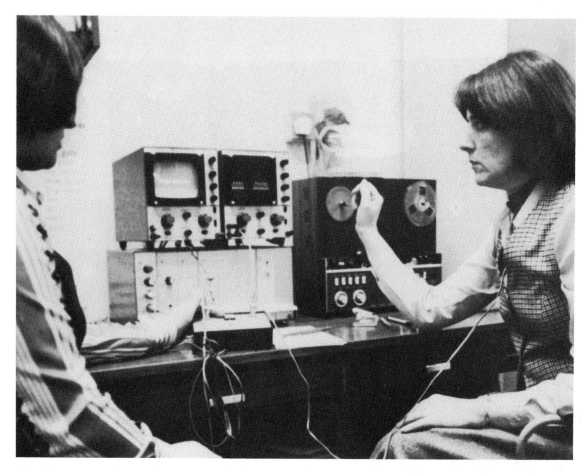

The equipment on this bench is used to help very deaf people improve the way they speak. When the deaf person speaks, the sound waves can be displayed on the screen of a cathode ray tube (see book 5 page 28). The picture is used by a specially trained person called a speech therapist to show the deaf person where the voice needs to be changed in order for the words to be spoken more clearly.

The outer ear

The *pinna* is made from cartilage and is covered with skin. It directs sound waves towards the auditory canal.

The *auditory canal* is about 2.5 cm long. It is lined with hairs and wax-making cells. The hairs and wax help to trap dust particles and keep the eardrum clean.

The *eardrum* is a very thin membrane of skin which stretches over the inner end of the auditory canal. When a sound wave reaches the ear it makes the eardrum move in and out a little, or vibrate (see page 28). The eardrum vibrates at the same frequency as the sound. A loud sound makes the eardrum vibrate more strongly than a quiet sound.

The middle ear

Air pressure control. The middle ear is a space filled with air. The eustachian tube is connected to the throat in such a way that, every time we swallow, air can enter or leave the middle ear. This air movement keeps the air in the middle ear at the same pressure as the air outside the head. If there was a difference in air pressure the eardrum could not vibrate properly and some deafness would be caused.

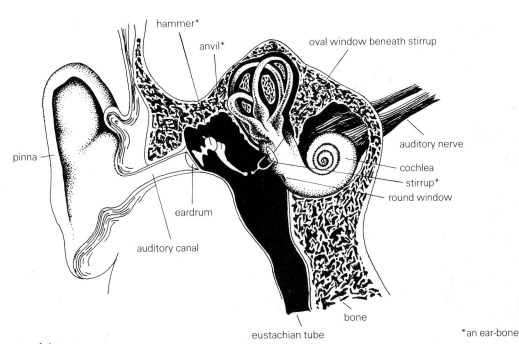

hammer*

anvil*

oval window beneath stirrup

auditory nerve

cochlea

stirrup*

round window

pinna

eardrum

auditory canal

bone

eustachian tube

*an ear-bone

62 The parts of the ear

Ear-bones. The vibrations of the eardrum are passed along the ear-bones to the oval window. The ear-bones are connected to each other so that they act like levers. One end of the hammer receives a small movement from the eardrum. The other end of the hammer passes a larger movement to one end of the anvil, and this in turn passes a larger movement to the stirrup. This lever action increases the force of the vibrations by twenty times and gives enough power to the stirrup for it to tap on the oval window and make the liquid in the inner ear vibrate.

The inner ear

The space in the inner ear is filled with a watery liquid. The vibrations from the oval window pass into the liquid in the cochlea. This is a tube about 3.5 cm long, which is coiled up a like a snail shell. Inside the cochlea are thousands of tiny hairs which are arranged like rungs in a ladder. Each hair moves up and down when a vibration of a certain frequency reaches it. The lowest frequency which makes a hair vibrate is 16 hertz. The highest frequency at which a hair vibrates is 20 kilohertz.

When a hair vibrates it makes the end of a nerve fibre produce an electrical message or impulse. This message travels along the fibre and through the auditory nerve to the brain and we hear the sound.

The vibrations in the liquid in the cochlea eventually reach the round window and make it vibrate too. The purpose of the round window is to release the pressure of these vibrations back into the air. If this pressure were not released the cochlea would not be able to work properly.

Deafness

Deafness can be caused by (1) a hole forming in the eardrum, (2) the ear-bones sticking together and (3) damage to the nerve fibres carrying the messages to the brain.

Further reading

TOPIC	BOOK	PAGE
The eye	6	18
Sound	6	28
Noise	6	38

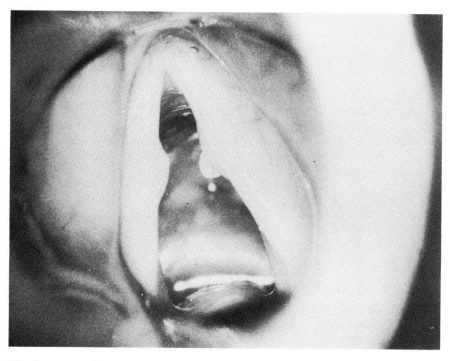

The human voice
The vocal cords

This photograph shows the inside of the voice box or larynx. It was taken using optical fibres (see

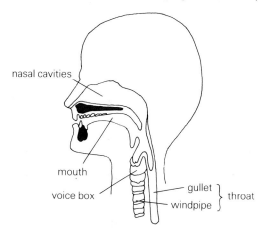

63 The position of the voice box

64 The vocal cords

page 20). Diagram 63 shows the position of the voice box in the neck. The A-shaped opening seen in the photograph is made by the vocal cords. They are the flaps of tissue on either side of the opening. When you are not speaking small muscles in the wall of the voice box pull the cords apart, as can be seen here, but when you are speaking the cords move closer together, as shown in diagram 64.

Making a sound

The vocal cords vibrate when air rushes through the narrow gap between them. Which way is the air moving when you speak – into your lungs or out of them? Breathe and speak to find out. The vibrations make sound waves, which pass through the air spaces in your throat, mouth and nasal cavities (see diagram 63). The air inside these spaces vibrates, too, as the sound waves pass through them. These vibrations affect the sound waves made by the vocal cords.

The way the air vibrates depends on the size and shape of the spaces. As the size and shape of the air spaces in your head is different from those of everyone else, the vibration of the air in them helps to give your voice its special sound.

Bird song

In most birds the voice is made by the syrinx (see diagram 65). To make a sound, the bird must first use some of its muscles to squeeze air from its air sacs, through the lungs and into the right and left bronchi. The bird can control the opening and closing of these two tubes. If just one tube is open – the left bronchus, for example – air will rush over one membrane in the syrinx and make it vibrate. This vibration makes the bird song. If the bird opens both bronchi, the two membranes in the syrinx vibrate and the bird sings a duet!

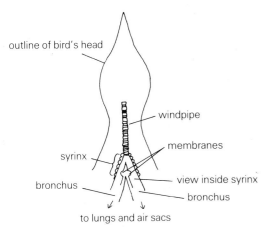

65 The syrinx in a bird

The hissing snake

The hissing sound is made by air as it is forced through the opening at the end of the windpipe, into the back of the mouth.

The croaking frog (diagram 66)

When a frog is about to croak it fills two pouches with air. These pouches each have an opening into the mouth. When a frog makes a sound with its voice box, the sound waves cause the air in the pouches to vibrate. The vibrating air makes the croaking sound louder.

Insect sounds (diagram 67)

Many insects, such as the bee and mosquito, move their wings rapidly up and down when they fly. These movements of the wings make a humming sound. A cricket has a file and scraper on its wings, as the diagram shows. When the insect rubs its wings together, the scraper moves across the file and makes a clicking sound. The death watch beetle (see book 4 page 35) makes a tapping sound by knocking its head against the wood on which it is standing.

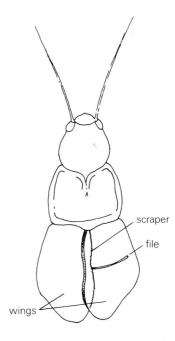

67 The file and scraper on a cricket's wings

66 Air pouches of a frog

Further reading

TOPIC	BOOK	PAGE
Sound	6	28
Musical instruments	6	34
Birds and flight	1	18

MUSICAL INSTRUMENTS

If you hit a triangle, then touch it, you will feel a tingle as you stop the metal vibrating. It is the vibration which makes the musical sound. Most instruments make musical sounds either by being blown (wind instruments) or by having their strings plucked or scraped (stringed instruments).

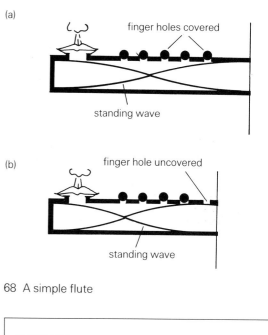

(a)
finger holes covered
standing wave

(b)
finger hole uncovered
standing wave

68 A simple flute

GLOSSARY

standing wave: a wave which remains in one place. The vibrations in the wave are passed to the rest of the instrument and make it vibrate to produce progressive waves (see page 28).

Wind instruments

To make the musical note, the air inside the wind instrument is made to vibrate. The vibrating air makes a standing wave. The speed at which the wave vibrates (called its frequency) makes the pitch of the note.

In the flute, for example, the air is made to vibrate by blowing across the mouthpiece. When all the holes in the side of the flute are covered up, the tube of air inside the instrument is long and a standing wave is made, as shown in diagram 68(a). When a hole on the flute is opened (diagram 68b), the tube of air inside the instrument becomes shorter. This makes the length of the standing wave shorter, so that its frequency increases and the pitch of the note rises. By opening and closing the holes on the flute, the flautist can play the notes on the sheet of music.

Reed instruments

A reed is a piece of cane in the mouthpiece of the instrument. When the player blows the reed, it vibrates and makes a standing wave in the column of air in the instrument. The clarinet has one reed and the oboe and bassoon have two. are example

69 A trombone

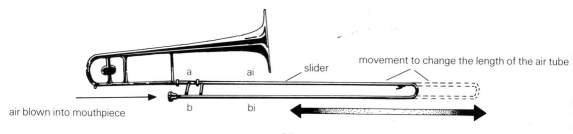

a   ai   slider   movement to change the length of the air tube

air blown into mouthpiece   b   bi

Brass instruments

The lips of the musician are used to make the air vibrate in a brass instrument. The length of the standing wave may be changed by altering the length of the air tube, as shown in the diagram of a trombone. *+rombone is an example*

The mouthpiece is connected to a tube which ends at bi. A bar from b to a connects this tube to another one which ends at ai. The slider is a U-shaped tube which fits over the other tubes at a-ai and b-bi. When the musician wishes to increase the length of the tube of air inside the instrument the second bar is pushed to the right and the slider moves over the two other tubes towards ai and bi. The dotted line shows the new position of the slider and the extra length of air tube that is made.

Stringed instruments

When a stretched string is plucked, as in the playing of a guitar, or scraped, as in the playing of a violin, it vibrates, as shown in diagram 70. A range of notes can be played on the instrument just by having stretched strings with different weights. In the guitar in the photograph the heaviest string is at the top. It vibrates more slowly than the others and makes the lowest-pitched sound. The lightest string is at the bottom. It makes the highest-pitched sound.

The wave on a string can be made shorter by pressing part of the string against the neck of the guitar, as shown in the photograph. This action raises the pitch of the note made by the string.

The vibrating string makes the air around it vibrate (see page 28). The vibrations pass to the air inside the body of the instrument (beneath this player's right arm) and make it vibrate, too. These extra vibrations make the sound louder.

Harmonics

Harmonics are sometimes called overtones. When an instrument makes a note, a long sound wave called a fundamental is formed, as shown in diagrams 68 and 70. Shorter waves called harmonics or overtones (diagram 71) are made, too. Each type of instrument makes harmonics which are different from those of other instruments. When two instruments, such as the flute and the guitar, are playing the same note, we hear two different sounds. This difference is due to the harmonics made by each instrument.

string moves up and down between these two positions

70 Vibration of a plucked string

71 (a) Vibration of the second harmonic

71 (b) Vibrations of a plucked string (fundamental and second harmonic together)

second harmonic vibration

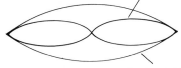

fundamental vibration

Further reading

TOPIC	BOOK	PAGE
Sound	6	28
The ear	6	30
Microphones	6	36

The instrument in the photograph below is used to measure the amount of sound that is made in a factory. When sound waves strike the microphone at the tip of the metal arm, a current of electricity is made to flow through the electronic circuits in the instrument. This current makes the needle move across the scale on the meter and the loudness of the sound can be measured.

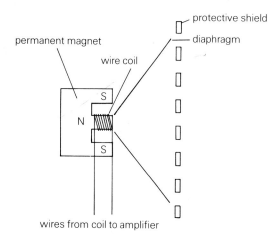

permanent magnet

wire coil

protective shield

diaphragm

wires from coil to amplifier

72 The moving coil microphone

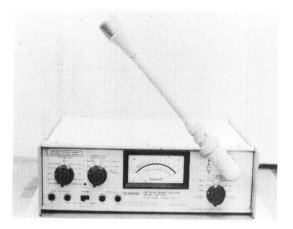

Types of microphone

Three of the most widely used types of microphone are the moving coil type, the ribbon type and the carbon type.

The moving coil microphone (diagram 72) is used to record the loud sounds made by drums and electric guitars. It is not easily damaged by wind and rain and is used in outside broadcasts. When a sound wave strikes the diaphragm (see diagram), it pushes the diaphragm to the left, then pulls it to the right. The coil attached to the diaphragm moves backwards and forwards through the magnetic field. This makes an electric current in the wire in the coil (see book 5 page 12).

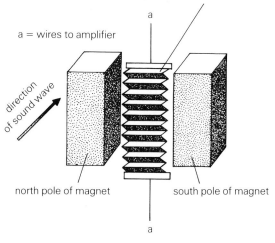

very thin sheet of aluminium foil

a

a = wires to amplifier

direction of sound wave

north pole of magnet

south pole of magnet

a

73 The main parts of a ribbon microphone

The ribbon microphone (diagram 73) is used to record high-pitched sounds or sounds made by a wide range of instruments playing together – as in an orchestra, for example. The sound waves make the very thin diaphragm move backwards and forwards in the magnetic field and generate a current of electricity.

The carbon microphone is used in telephones (see book 5 page 22).

Making a sound

The most common type of loudspeaker is the moving coil loudspeaker, shown in diagram 74. It is fitted to radio and television sets, cassette recorders, record players and is used in public address systems in theatres, sports stadiums and supermarkets.

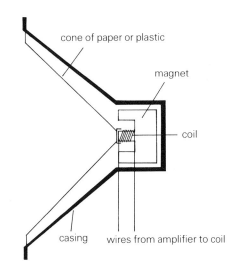

74 The moving coil loudspeaker

The sounds to be broadcast reach the loudspeaker in the form of pulses of electric current (see book 5 pages 26 and 32, and page 36 here). When a pulse of electricity from the amplifier passes through the coil, it makes a magnetic field around the wire. The magnetic fields of the coil and the magnet make a force which moves the coil and the cone. This movement makes the cone push and pull on the air around it and send out sound waves, as described on page 28.

The photograph here shows two loudspeaker cabinets. On the right, the front of the cabinet has been removed, so that you can see the position of the loudspeakers. The smaller speaker (known as the "tweeter") makes the high-pitched sounds and the larger speaker (known as the "woofer") makes the middle- and low-pitched sounds.

Further reading

NOISE

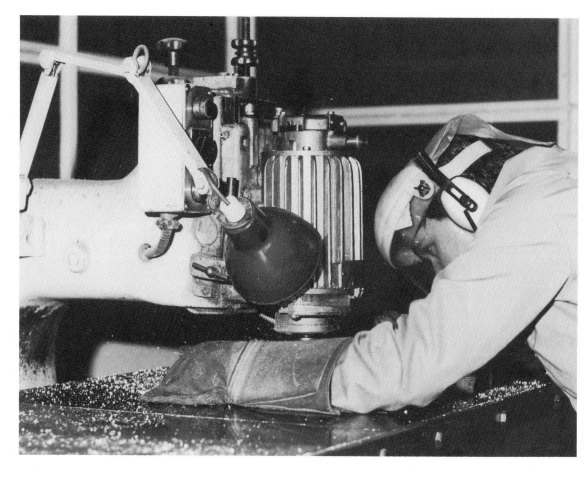

75 Wave form of a voice or musical sound

76 Wave form of a drill or scraping sound

The sound made by a voice or a musical instrument has a smooth wave form, as diagram 75 shows. The sound coming from the metal drill in the photograph is rather like that made by dragging a chair across a classroom floor. It has a wave form like that shown in diagram 76. Sounds with a wave form like this are usually called noises – although sometimes you may think that voices and musical instruments are making a noise, too.

Measuring loudness

Sometimes a sound could be called a noise because it is too loud. Scientists use the decibel scale (see table 2) to measure the loudness of a noise. Sounds above 90 decibels can damage the ears. In factories where noisy machinery, like the drill, is being used, the sound level is checked by using a meter like the one shown on page 36.

Decibels	Examples
140	The sound hurts
130	Jet aircraft taking off
120	–
110	A road drill (see book 1 page 29)
100	–
90	A class without a teacher
80	Vacuum cleaner
70	–
60	A busy department store
50	Normal speech is 55 decibels
40	Voices in a town at night
30	–
20	Whisper
10	Rustling leaves
0	–

Table 2   The decibel scale

Noise and health

Noisy surroundings make it difficult for people to think properly, or relax. Working in very noisy surroundings can eventually lead to permanent ear damage.

While the engineer in the photograph is working close to the drill he wears ear-muffs to protect his ears and help him to concentrate.

The reflection of sound

The moving particles in a sound wave are given their energy by a vibrating object, as described on page 28. When the sound wave strikes the surface of a wall, for example, some of the energy of the air particles is absorbed by the material in the wall and some of it makes a sound wave which is reflected back into the air.

The noisy classroom

When a sound wave strikes a hard, smooth wall, most of the energy produces a reflected wave which is only a little weaker than the original one. The extra sound made by the reflected waves makes a slight echo called a reverberation. In a room full of hard surfaces, such as a classroom, the reflected sound waves may raise the sound level by nearly 10 decibels.

Home furnishings

Most of the energy in a sound wave is absorbed when it strikes a soft, rough surface, and only a little energy is then used to make a reflected wave. Wallpaper, carpets, curtains and furniture absorb a great deal of energy in sound waves and help to keep the noise level down.

The silencer (diagram 77)

A petrol or diesel engine gets its power from the energy that is released by exploding air and petrol vapour together. These explosions (see book 5 page 39) take place in the engine's cylinders and the waste gases that are made pass out of the engine with a great deal of force. The waste gases push on the air particles and make them vibrate strongly, to produce a loud noise.

When a silencer is fitted to the engine (diagram 77), the waste gases lose some of their energy every time they strike a baffle, and change direction, so that eventually they have little energy left to push on the air as they leave the tailpipe.

Further reading

TOPIC	BOOK	PAGE
Sound	6	28
Air pollution	1	42
Water pollution	2	18
Habitat destruction	7	36

77 Inside a car silencer

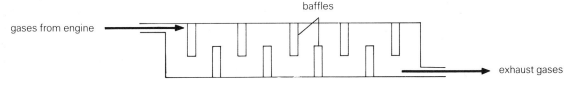

gases from engine → baffles → exhaust gases

When a sound wave strikes a flat surface, such as a wall, it is reflected in a similar way to a light ray, as shown on page 6.

Echoes and distance

You have probably made an echo at some time. Perhaps you have shouted or clapped your hands at a wall or cliff face (diagram 78). For you to hear the echo there must be a time interval of 0.1 seconds between your clap or shout and the reflected sound reaching your ears. As sound travels at about 330 metres per second – 33 metres in 0.1 second – the distance for the sound to travel must be at least 34 metres.

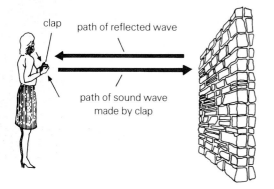

78 A sound and its echo

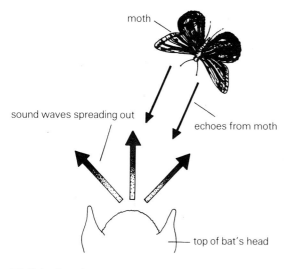

79 Echo location

Echo location (diagram 79)

Most bats find their food by using echoes. They make short pulses of ultrasonic sound waves which pass out from the bat's head, as the diagram shows.

The bat can judge the distance and position of an insect from the way the reflected waves return to its ears. If the echo returns quickly, the moth is near; if the echo returns slowly, the moth is further away. A moth on the right of the bat will send an echo which reaches its right ear first. If the moth is on the left, the echo will reach the left ear first. How would the bat know if the moth was straight ahead?

Dolphins use echoes to find food in a similar way to the bat. The oil-bird and the swiftlet are two kinds of bird which nest in deep caves. They make clicking sounds and use the echoes from the cave walls to help them fly in almost total darkness.

GLOSSARY

pulse of ultrasonic sound waves: a small number of sound waves which are released one after another. They form a group called a pulse.

Echo sounder (diagram 80)

Echo sounding equipment can be used in the following way to find the depth of water beneath a ship. A pulse of ultrasonic sound waves is released from the transducer (see page 42) and the echo is collected by a receiver. By measuring the time between the release of the pulse of sound waves and the echo being received, the distance from the sea bed can be calculated and displayed.

Uses of echo sounders

Echo sounders are used (1) to help the crew move a ship through shallow water, (2) to help geologists make a survey of the sea bed, (3) to help trawler crews find shoals of fish (see book 7 page 21).

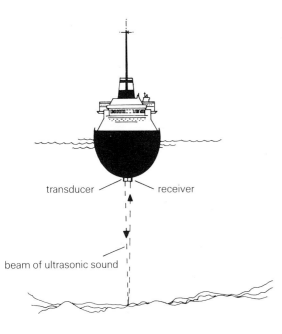

transducer — receiver

beam of ultrasonic sound

80 Echo sounding

SONAR

SOund Navigation And Ranging is used by ships in the Navy to detect submarines. The transducer can be moved to direct its sound waves over a wide area beneath the ship.

The anechoic chamber

Reflected sounds add to the noise of our everyday life, as described on page 39. When a new microphone or loudspeaker is being tested, there must not be any reflected sound waves around it to interfere with the tests. In the photograph, the telephone handset being set up on the model contains both a microphone and loudspeaker (see book 5 page 22). The wedges covering the walls of this room absorb almost all the sound that reaches them – making the room free from echoes. This type of test room is called an anechoic chamber.

Further reading

TOPIC	BOOK	PAGE
Sound	6	28
Ultrasonics	6	42
Jets	1	24
Navigation	2	26
Radar	5	30

Ultrasonic sound waves have a frequency (see page 4) greater than 20 kilohertz and cannot be heard by human ears. The bat and dolphin, mentioned on page 40, make ultrasonic sound waves and have ears to hear them. Dogs can hear some ultrasonic sounds, but cannot make them.

Making ultrasonic sound (diagram 81)

When an alternating current (see book 5 page 13) is passed through a special kind of crystal, this changes shape, as the diagram shows. The changes in shape of the crystal make the air particles vibrate, as shown in diagram 58 on page 28, but the movements are so fast that an ultrasonic sound wave is produced. A piece of equipment which makes ultrasonic waves is called a transducer.

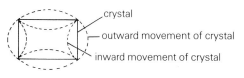

crystal

outward movement of crystal

inward movement of crystal

both movements greatly enlarged

81 Making ultrasonic sound

Uses of ultrasonics

Non-destructive testing. The inside of the metal bar in the photograph is being examined for cracks and cavities. The transducer and receiver are in the cylinder on the top of the bar. Whenever they strike a hole, the ultrasonic waves from the transducer are reflected to the receiver. The receiver converts the energy in the echo into an electrical impulse, which makes a spike on the screen.

Body scanners (diagram 82). If a beam of ultrasonic waves is passed through the body, the different parts, such as the bones, fat and muscles, reflect the sound waves in different ways. These reflections are collected and displayed on a television screen in such a way that the inside of the body can be seen.

Some scanners use X rays instead of ultrasonic waves. The X rays can be dangerous to a developing baby and so, when a pregnant woman is being examined, harmless ultrasonic waves are always used.

television screen showing position of baby

transducer/receiver

82 An ultrasonic body scanner

Drills. If a transducer is attached to a drill in a special way, the ultrasonic waves can be used to make the drill move rapidly up and down. A normal household drill spins round and makes a circular hole, but the motion of an ultrasonic drill allows a wide range of hole shapes to be cut.

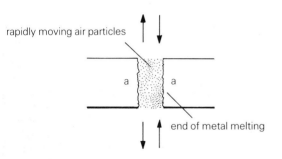

rapidly moving air particles

a   a

end of metal melting

a = surfaces of metal to be welded

83 Heating surface with ultrasonic sound

Welding (diagram 83). The air particles carrying an ultrasonic wave move very fast. When an ultrasonic wave passes between two materials, as the diagram shows, the moving air particles rub across the surfaces of the materials and heat them up. The hot surfaces can then be joined together. Ultrasonic waves are used to weld the metal connections of an electronic circuit to a microchip (see book 5 page 41), or to weld together two metals or two plastics.

Cleaning (diagram 84). Many pieces of industrial equipment have parts which are difficult to clean with detergents. When a dirty piece of equipment is placed in water, and a beam of ultrasonic waves is passed through the liquid, tiny spaces form, as the diagram shows. Each space contains a small vacuum (see book 1 page 30) which sucks a dirt particle off the surface of the equipment.

Further reading

TOPIC	BOOK	PAGE
Sound	6	28
Echoes	6	40
Using air gases	1	34
Solvents and detergents	2	42

84 Removing dirt from a surface

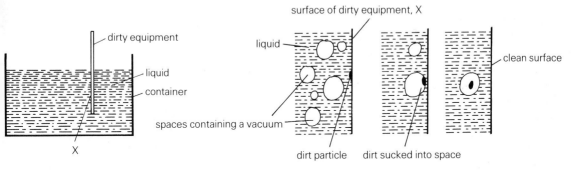

dirty equipment

liquid

container

X

spaces containing a vacuum

surface of dirty equipment, X

liquid

clean surface

dirt particle   dirt sucked into space

(a) Arrangement of the equipment

(b) Highly magnified view

A TIME SCALE OF SCIENTIFIC DISCOVERY AND INVENTION

BC

c. 2,500 Egyptians used mirrors.

c. 400 Greeks used concave and convex mirrors.

AD

2–66 Seneca (Greece) described how glass bowls filled with water could be used to magnify objects. He also identified the colours in a rainbow.

139 Claudius Ptolemy (Greece) made investigations on refraction (see page 8).

965–1038 Al Hazan (Arabia) described the parts of the eye and made a drawing of them. His work was translated into Latin in 1572 and it was at this time that the words retina, cornea and humors were used (see page 18).

1278 Witelo (Greece) explained how stars twinkled (see book 3 page 4).

1280–85 The lens was invented by an unknown person in Italy. (The word "lens" comes from the Italian word for lentil – which is the shape of a convex lens.) The first spectacles were also made at about this time.

1590–1609 Z. Janssen (Holland) made the first microscope.

1608 H. Lippershay (Holland) constructed the first telescope.

1610 Galileo Galilei (Italy) made the first scientific discoveries with a telescope. He examined the moon, satellites of Jupiter and sunspots (see book 3 page 6).

1665 R. Hooke (UK) described light moving as if it were made from waves.

1666 I. Newton (UK) showed that the white light of the sun was made from seven different colours (see page 8).

1668 I. Newton (UK) designed and built the first reflecting telescope.

1672 I. Newton (UK) put forward the theory that light waves are made up from particles called corpuscles.

1676 O. Römer (Denmark) discovered that light travelled at a certain speed by studying the movement of one of Jupiter's moons.

1678 C. Huygens (Holland) described light as moving with a wave-like motion.

1728 J. Bradley (UK) calculated that light travelled from the sun to the earth in just over eight minutes.

1752 T. Melvill (UK) was the first to see that each element made its own spectrum (see page 8).

1758 J. Dollond (UK) found that by joining different kinds of lenses together, better images could be made.

1801 W. Wollaston (UK) invented the spectroscope.

1811 E.L. Malus (France) discovered polarized light.

1815 A.J. Fresnel (France) began experiments which showed that light moved with a wave-like motion.

c. 1816 J.P. Biot (France) discovered that a mineral called tourmaline could be used to make polarized light. He also discovered that polarized light could be used to identify minerals.

1816 J.N. Nièpces (France) made the first camera but had difficulty making permanent photographs.

1823 J. Fraunhofer (Austria) measured the wavelength of light using a diffraction grating – an instrument which separates the light waves in a beam so that light of each wavelength can be seen on its own.

1830 L.J.M. Daguerre (France) discovered a way of making a permanent photograph (one that did not fade away).

1834–35 W.H. Fox Talbot (UK) made experiments in photography.

1842 C. Doppler (Austria) described how sound waves produced the changing sounds made by objects that pass by (see page 29).

1850 J.L. Fourcault (France) experimented on the speed of light and showed that it travelled more slowly in glass than in air.

1851 H. Helmholtz (Germany) invented the ophthalmoscope – an instrument for studying the inside of the eye.

1859 G. Kirchoff (Germany) discovered that each element could be recognized by the spectrum that it makes (see page 8).

1860–61 R.W. Bunsen (Germany) and G. Kirchoff (Germany) discovered the metals caesium and rubidium by making studies with a spectroscope.

1864 J. Clerk Maxwell (UK) worked out a theory which showed that light was made from electro-magnetic waves (see page 4).

1878 D.E. Hughes (UK) invented the carbon microphone (see book 5 page 22).

1880s P. Curie (France) showed how to make ultrasonic waves by passing electricity through a special kind of crystal (see page 42).

1887 E.A. Frisch (Germany) made the first contact lenses.

GLOSSARY

contact lens: a thin lens made from glass or plastic which is worn on the front of the eye and is used to help people with poor sight to see more clearly.

1888 G. Eastman (USA) invented the roll of film for cameras.

1897 At Yerkes Observatory, Wisconsin, (USA), the largest refracting telescope was built.

1900 P. Lenard (Germany) explained how zinc became electrically charged after ultraviolet light had been shining on it. He said the light knocked electrons out of the metal's atoms. (See book 5 page 4.)

1900 M. Plank (Germany) put forward the idea that all kinds of radiation (see page 4) were made from small packets of energy. He called each packet a quantum. Packets of light energy became known as photons.

1905 A. Einstein (USA) worked out his theory of special relativity which explained how light could be thought of as being made from waves and photons.

1916 P. Langevin (France) made ultrasonic waves in water and detected their echo. His work led to the making of echo sounders.

1934	P. Shaw (UK) invented the cat's-eye reflector for use on roads.
1935	Kodak (USA) introduced a multi-layered colour film called kodachrome.
1936	Bell Telephone Laboratories (USA) developed a machine which could recognize a human voice.
1938	C.F. Carlson (USA) discovered how to make photocopies. Photocopying machines were developed from his discoveries.
1946	Ultrasonic echo sounders were used to find shoals of fish.
1948	D. Gabor (Hungary) described how holograms might be made. (See also 1960.)
1948	E. Land (USA) introduced his polaroid camera.
1955	N. Kapary (UK) made optical fibres.
1957	Marconi Limited (USA) introduced a navigation system using the Doppler effect (see page 28) for aircraft.
1960	T. Maiman (USA) invented the laser. This could now be used to make holograms.
1962	Bell Telephone Laboratories (USA) reflected a laser off the moon's surface.
1963	Kodak (USA) introduced a camera loaded with a cartridge of film – the instamatic camera.
1964	Dr Stookey (USA) invented photochrom light-sensitive glasses. They are made from silica (see book 4 page 5) and silver particles.
1971	Hughes Aircraft Co. (USA) used holograms to test aircraft wings.
1974	University of Texas (USA) developed a holographic electron microscope which can show the electron cloud of an atom (see also book 5 page 4).
1977	Bell Telephone Co. (USA) used optical fibres to transmit television signals.
1982	Kodak (USA) introduced the disc camera which uses film mounted on a disc.

BOOK LIST

Allen, J., *Tricks of the light and its practical uses*, Piccadilly Press, 1985

Desoutter, D.M., *Your book of sound*, Faber and Faber, 1971

Griffiths, J., *Lasers and Holograms* (Exploration and Discovery series), Macmillan, 1983

Gunston, W.T., *Your book of light*, Faber and Faber, 1969

Hardy, D.A., *Light and Sight* (The advance of science series), World's Work, 1977

Kurth, H., *Echolocation*, World's Work, 1976

Myring, L. and Kimmit, M., *Lasers*, Usborne Publishing Ltd, 1984

Riley, P.D., *Looking at Microscopes* (Looking at Science series), Batsford Educational, 1985

Wicks, K., *Sound and Recording* (Understanding Science series), Longman, 1982

PROJECTS

Using Book 6 only

A Light

1 (a) What are the seven colours in the light from the sun?
page 4
(b) Which colour has (i) the shortest wavelength, (ii) the longest wavelength?
page 4
(c) Has green light a longer or shorter wavelength than blue light?
page 4
2 Who discovered that white light could be split up into seven different colours, and when?
page 44
3 (a) What has been added to a prism in a spectroscope to make a better spectrum?
page 8
(b) What is an optical spectrograph used for?
page 8
(c) What is used to examine the spectrum made in a spectrograph?
page 8
4 (a) Make a drawing of the eye, using diagram 36 on page 18 to help you. On your drawing label the conjunctiva, cornea, lens, retina and iris.
(b) On the diagram mark (i) an A where you would find a liquid which provides nourishment to the eye, (ii) a B where you would find jelly, (iii) a C where you would find cone cells, and (iv) a D where you would find rod cells.
(c) Which of the features A,B,C or D send electrical messages to the brain when light shines on them? page 18
5 How is light in a laser beam different from a beam of ordinary light?
page 26

B Reflections

1 (a) Draw a picture of four light rays striking a rough surface and making a diffuse reflection.
page 6
(b) Name four surfaces around you which make diffuse reflections.
page 6
2 (a) What kind of reflection takes place on a mirror's surface?
page 6
(b) How is a concave mirror different from a convex mirror? Which one gives you (i) a wide field of view, (ii) a magnified image?
page 7
3 What is the purpose of a mirror in (a) a telescope, (b) a microscope, (c) a camera, (d) making a hologram, (e) making a laser? pages 10, 12, 14, 20 and 26
4 Make a list of all the mirrors in your home (include cars and bike, etc). For each one, state whether the mirror is flat, concave or convex.
5 (a) Who invented the cat's-eye reflector, and when?
page 44
(b) Where would you find cat's-eye reflectors and how do you think they are useful?
6 (a) What kind of surface is best for reflecting sound waves?
page 39
(b) What kinds of surface are found in most bathrooms?
(c) Use the answers from (a) and (b) to explain why you think people sing in the bath.

C Lenses

1 When was the first lens invented and how did it get its name?
page 44
2 How is a convex lens different from a concave lens? page 9
3 Lens D in diagram 25 on page 14 is called a plano-convex lens because of its shape. How is it different from a convex and a concave lens?

4 What kind of lenses are found in (i) an astronomical telescope, (ii) a pair of opera glasses, (iii) a pair of spectacles for curing (a) short sight, (b) long sight?
pages 10, 19
5 Describe how the lens in the eye changes shape when you are looking at (i) a book, (ii) out of the window. page 19
6 Who invented the following instruments and when: (a) the camera, (b) the spectroscope, (c) the microscope, (d) the telescope?
page 44

D The eye and the camera

1 Make a drawing of the eye seen from the front, as in the photograph on page 18. Label the sclerotic, iris and pupil.
page 18
2 Which of the five transparent parts of the eye are found in front of the iris?
page 18
3 Make a drawing of the eye seen from the front when it is looking about in (a) a dark room, (b) bright sunlight.
page 18
4 What is a contact lens and when was it invented? page 44
5 (a) What is the purpose of a shutter on a camera? page 14
(b) How is the shutter on an adjustable camera different from the shutter on a simple camera? page 14
(c) What part of the camera works like (a) the iris, (b) the retina?
pages 14 and 18
6 The following people made important contributions to the development of photography – J.N. Nièpces, G. Eastman, W.H. Fox Talbot, E. Land, L.J.M. Daguerre. Arrange their achievements in the order in which they were made. State the achievement each person made.
page 44

E Sound

1 What happens to the particles in the air when a vibrating body (a) pushes on them, (b) pulls away from them?
page 28
2 (a) Rule a line 8 cm long. Draw four complete wavelengths along the line, using diagram 1 on page 4 to help you.
(b) Rule another 8 cm line and draw a wave pattern which has a higher frequency than the first diagram. page 28
3 If the 8 cm line stands for the distance covered by the waves in one second, what is the frequency in hertz of the waves in (i) the first diagram, (ii) the second diagram?
pages 4 and 28
4 Why does the sound from an ambulance siren change the pitch of its note as it rushes by?
page 29
5 What makes the vibrations in the air when (a) a human talks, (b) a bird sings, (c) a cricket calls?
page 32

F Making a sound

1 Draw two pictures of a head showing the air passages. (Use diagram 63 on page 32 to help you). (a) In the first picture show the direction of the sound waves from the voice box when a person is speaking. (b) In the second picture show the direction of the sound waves when a person is humming.
page 32
2 What helps to make your voice have its own special sound?
page 32
3 When and where was a machine first made that could recognize a human voice?
page 44
4 What makes the air vibrate in (a) the flute, (b) the oboe, (c) the trombone?
page 34

5 (a) What is a "tweeter" and where would you find it?
page 37
(b) What parts of a loudspeaker move when a pulse of electricity passes through it? page 37
6 Why does a silencer with a hole in it make a loud sound? Draw a diagram (using diagram 77 page 39 to help you) to explain your answer. page 39

Using Book 6 and other books in the series

G The microscope

1 Make a drawing of the microscope in the photograph on page 13 and label the parts using diagram 23 on page 13 to help you. In what ways is the microscope in the photograph different from the one in the diagram? Book 6 page 13
2 How is the microscope on page 5 different from the one on page 13?
3 If you examined pollen grains with a microscope, how could you tell (a) pine pollen from hazel pollen? (b) grass pollen from sycamore pollen? (c) pine pollen from sycamore pollen? Book 1 page 14
4 If you were to examine water life with a microscope,
(a) What types of diatom might you see?
(b) How could you tell (i) amoeba from a ciliate? (ii) a rotifer from Cyclops? Book 2 page 10
5 What can you see in a piece of leather when it is examined with a microscope? Book 4 page 22
6 How is an electron microscope different from a microscope which uses light? Book 5 page 34

H Making and playing a record

1 (a) What kind of wave is made in a wind instrument when you blow it? Book 6 page 34

(b) How does the instrument make a progressive wave?
Book 6 pages 28 and 34
2 What kind of microphone would you use to record the high-pitched sound of a flute? How does the microphone work?
Book 6 page 36
3 How is the sound recorded onto audio tape?
Book 5 page 32
4 (a) How is a record made?
(b) Make a drawing of a groove of a record that would make a loud, high-frequency sound.
(c) How are pulses of electricity made when a stylus moves along a groove? Book 5 page 33
5 (a) What makes a loudspeaker make a sound?
(b) Which loudspeaker would make the sound of the flute – the "tweeter" or the "woofer"? Book 6 page 37

I Plants and food

1 What is happening at the centre of the sun? Book 3 page 6
2 What are the different kinds of electromagnetic waves given out by the sun? Book 6 page 4
3 Which kind of electromagnetic waves are used by the plant to make food? Book 6 page 22
4 What is chlorophyll and where is it found? Book 6 page 22
5 (a) What is the name of the process in which a root hair takes up water?
(b) What happens to the water after it has got into the root hair cell?
(c) What happens to most water that enters the leaf?
Book 2 page 30
6 How is the energy from light used in a leaf? Book 6 page 22
7 Name the parts of the respiratory system that carbon dioxide passes through, from the blood in your lungs to the air around your head. Book 1 page 33
8 What happens to the carbon dioxide in a leaf?
Book 6 page 22
9 What is the name of the process by which plants make food in their leaves? Book 6 page 22

INDEX